THE JOURNEY TO FINDING YOURSELF

THE JOURNEY TO FINDING YOURSELF

Rena Camille

iUniverse, Inc.
Bloomington

The Journey to Finding Yourself

iUniverse books may be ordered through booksellers or by contacting:

iUniverse
1663 Liberty Drive
Bloomington, IN 47403
www.iuniverse.com
1-800-Authors (1-800-288-4677)

ISBN: 978-1-4759-0612-7 (sc)
ISBN: 978-1-4759-0613-4 (ebk)

Printed in the United States of America

iUniverse rev. date: 03/19/2012

The evolution of women continues.

We will not be defeated.

DEDICATION

This book is dedicated to my girls! Emani, Emiya and Ja'Miyah! I love you three endlessly; everything I do is for you! Mommy loves you!

SPECIAL THANKS

Gino Harris photographer for "The Evolution of Woman" photo shoot

The Amazing lead Stylist: Tamera Simmons, showcasing her work on
facebook.com/tamera.simmons

Models: Rose James, Hannah Grimes, Valaira Sa-Ra

CONTENTS

Lesson 1: Mission Statement 1

Lesson 2: Relationships and Reality 4

Lesson 3: Health and Physical Issues 32

Lesson 4: Changing for the Better 38

Your Personal Journey 45

This is the beginning of your journey toward loving yourself and conquering low self-esteem. Low self-esteem shouldn't be looked at as a permanent inner disability, but minor lacerations that over time will heal, leaving only the memories of your trials and tribulations and a new confidence in how far you've come as a person.

The lessons in this book address the different stages that low self-esteem can take you through mentally, physically, spiritually, and emotionally. The objective is to identify the source of the problem, working from the core of the problem outward. This process is your ticket to bettering yourself. Countless women in America of all ages embark on this personal journey every day.

Some women do not develop low self-esteem until adulthood; many emotional burdens, such as those associated with an unhealthy marriage, weight gain, and aging, can cause their self-esteem to plummet. People in your everyday life, whether they are friends, family members, or complete strangers, can worsen how you feel about yourself with teasing, hurtful comments, and verbal or physical abuse. The way the people in your life treat you can affect your perception of your own value.

However, we all are in control of our own destiny and have the key to fixing our own self-esteem. Overcoming your inner obstacles will take determination and willpower, but you can do it. I'm not a professional psychologist, but a woman who has lived through this—who along the way found the secrets to achieving victory in the battle with low self-esteem.

"No one can make you feel inferior without your consent."—Eleanor Roosevelt

LESSON ONE

MISSION STATEMENT

Self-esteem:

1. *A realistic respect or favorable impression of oneself; self-respect.*
2. *An inordinately or exaggeratedly favorable impression of oneself.*

The first step to conquering low self-esteem is to realize that self-esteem originates within you. Outside parties may amplify your feelings of inadequacy, but those feelings still come from you. Blaming others for your issues is an attempt to avoid responsibility and to distract yourself from the root of the problem.

Low self-esteem causes you to be weak, sensitive, and vulnerable—states that can leave you susceptible to hurt feelings and irrational choices. Low self-esteem can cause us to criticize our own physical appearances or mental abilities. The American Society for Aesthetic Plastic Surgery started collecting statistics in 1997; a 2008 update showed that cosmetic procedures had skyrocketed 457 percent since then.[1] A 2007 study showed that 91 percent of the cosmetic procedures were performed on women of traditional racial and ethnic minorities. Botox injections, liposuction, and breast augmentation are only a few of the many procedures that women are undergoing to try to perfect themselves and gain self-confidence.

Physical appearance boils down not to inherent worth, but to genetics. You may have inherited a physical feature from one of your parents or grandparents that you find hideous, or you may be that sibling out of the bunch who has the "good hair." It's the luck of the draw, and those who

---

[1]   http://www.cosmeticplasticsurgerystatistics.com

feel as though they got the short end of the stick seek plastic surgery as the solution. The media promotes the importance of physical appearance and the supposed magic of cosmetic surgery. They may show a "before" picture of a small-breasted woman wearing no makeup and clad in an outfit only a grandmother would love. The "after" image might feature not only voluptuous breasts, but an outfit and makeup to die for. Such a comparison is not only skewed in its reality, but it also fails to disclose the dangers of the procedure, implying that cosmetic procedures are the easy path to perfection.

Many people who undergo plastic surgery encounter major and minor complications—and celebrities are not exempt. People need to be aware of the risks of plastic surgery: seroma (pocket of fluid in the body), hematoma (bruising), necrosis (tissue death), nerve injury, infection, hypertrophic scars (overly thick and sometimes painful scars), numbness, bleeding, ptosis (the drooping of the eyelid), and death. Celebrities like Kanye West understand the severity of cosmetic surgery; he lost his mother, Donda West, to the complications of plastic surgery.

Is a change in your physical appearance worth risking your life? The need for perfection can drive one to that point; but we have to decide what's more important: life, or the quick route to what we may perceive as perfection. A lot of people think that all women with low self-esteem are walking around in baggy clothing, staring down at the ground, taking no pride in themselves. But this book aims to shatter that stereotype, because many women who can afford the finer things in life still are not happy with what they see in the mirror. Even the most beautiful exterior cannot hide how a woman feels about herself.

For years, many dark-skinned women have felt that lighter-skinned women got more attention. Some darker skinned women felt that they didn't stand a chance against a woman who was light-skinned. Of course, there are a portion of dark-skinned women who embrace their skin tone and will be the first to yell, "The blacker the berry, the sweeter the juice!" However, there are some, dark-skinned women of all ages that suffer with self-esteem issues because they do not feel comfortable in their own skin. Way before our time, dark-skinned slaves in the South were treated differently than the light-skinned slaves. Light-skinned slaves were house servants, while the ones with darker skinned were condemned to the fields. The supposed reasoning was that those with lighter skin could have been relatives.

People today continue to assign importance to skin color. Some African American women and men bleach their skin in order to become lighter. The late Michael Jackson raised much controversy over whether he was bleaching his skin in order to become Caucasian, or if he truly had the skin disease vitiligo. Other celebrities are also said to be bleaching their skin, like the rapper Lil' Kim, but we have no way of knowing whether those allegations are true. Like other cosmetic procedures, bleaching the skin can be dangerous—it can increase the risk of cancer. Bleaching products were banned in France. Would you take the risk of using a product that a whole country has prohibited?

The first step is acknowledging that you have a condition. I call low self-esteem a condition because a condition is defined as "a particular mode of being of a person or thing" and an "existing state."

Some of your flaws—or, in some cases, supposed flaws—cannot be fixed. The only positive option is to embrace your flaws as a part of you. It's hard for someone else to completely love you, mind, body and soul, when you don't love yourself that much. A lot of times, women will look into a mirror to get a visual approval of their attire, finding much satisfaction in the exterior—all the while covering up their natural state. My suggestion is to stand or sit in front of a mirror in your natural state. While doing so, recite positive affirmations about yourself as a whole, but especially the areas that you have the most issues with. Positive energy does wonders; misery loves company, and negativity is its neighbor. Over time, you'll take steps to get closer to perfection, and while on that journey, you will start to embrace, love, and accept yourself for who you really are.

LESSON TWO

RELATIONSHIPS AND REALITY

Relationships take a lot of time and energy no matter what kind of relationship it is, it's hard work. If you have low self-esteem, the foundation of your relationships will not be as solid as it should be, and it could possibly crumble at any given moment. No one can fill the empty void inside of you; you have to fill it with your own love, and that may take time.

It's important to allow time to play its part; time heals everything. You may get impatient at times and become lonely; you might decide you would rather get in a relationship with someone first and work on you later. However, eventually that decision would prove to be a disaster. When you rush through any project, whether it's assembling furniture or studying for a test, you will eventually have to redo it if you care about the end results.

If you suspect you suffer from low self-esteem, answer the questions below to evaluate the strength of your foundation.

1. **Do you give more compliments to others than yourself, or do you find yourself feeling vulnerable and weak-minded around others?**

I believe it is important for you to compliment yourself as much, if not more, than you would your friends. It's easy to simply tell a friend, "You look nice." Tell yourself the same thing. Even if it's the only compliment you get all night, it should be as valued as the opinion of someone else. You want to get to a point where you do not need anyone else's validation that you look good—where even if not one person complimented you all

4

night, you'd still carry yourself as if every last person who approached you had commented on how amazing you looked. If you don't compliment yourself, it won't matter what anyone else has to say.

You can compliment yourself as many times as you feel is needed without saying a word aloud. Saying such things aloud too often will give people the wrong impression of you; your confidence-building efforts might come off as obnoxious vanity. The line between confidence and conceit is thin—make sure you stay on the right side of that line. Conceit will make you unappealing in the eyes of others. If you're arrogant or overly prideful about your looks or worth, all of your real friends will eventually stray, and you'll be left only with parasites that will stay with you as long as it's beneficial to them.

Low self-esteem can cause a parasite/host dynamic in romantic relationships as well. Many men will prey on weak women, manipulating the situation to get exactly what they want out of it. Parasites feed off their hosts, sometimes for a prolonged time; what started off as a scientific notion has become a part of our modern-day society. Some men will take advantage of women without remorse, even women who have kids, are disabled, or are at a bad point in life. These parasites will find your soft spot and completely manipulate it, giving you the love you feel you've never had, or being there for you when you feel as though everyone else has abandoned you. Being able to detect the wolves among the sheep is a very critical skill when you're undergoing surgery on your inner self.

2. Are you in a stable place in your life financially, physically, emotionally, and spiritually?

This question boils down to a simple yes or no answer. Excuses, justifications, and other avoidant tactics are unacceptable in this case. Stability is looked over, but there are women out there who developed low self-esteem or had their case of it worsen by not being able to get a job or possess the finer things in life.

3. If your man does something disrespectful or devastating to you, do you forgive him even though you know you should part ways?

If your spouse does something offensive enough that you have to contemplate whether to forgive him (or her), the best solution is to walk away. The break in the relationship may be temporary; as said before, time heals everything, and space may just be needed for a short time, so he can experience life without you. Forgiving him immediately or only allowing a couple of weeks to pass will only result in him deciding that what he's done is acceptable, and you can almost guarantee another daring act will occur in the future. In life, we fight for what we want, if we really want it; sometimes we even literally fight one another, which only makes women look ignorant, because the man is going to choose who he wants regardless of the outcome of such a fight.

If a man really wants you, he will do everything in his power to make the relationship work, even if it means allowing time apart to reconcile. If he can easily walk away, you weren't something worth fighting for, and it's best to let him go. In most cases, the man is the one ready to move on to the next relationship, while the woman ends up chasing behind him—even if he has done wrong. Women make it too easy for men to do what they like without fear of consequences. Women try to force love, when it's something that has to come naturally. Loving yourself first and putting your feelings first can set the tone for what you will and will not put up with.

4. Do you find yourself giving your friends advice despite your own bad position in life?

Friends and family will come to you for advice; life throws various obstacles in our path and it's normal to find comfort in confiding in one another. However, when a woman is going through low self-esteem and working on herself, I believe it is best to keep the advice to a minimum. In times in need, Bible verses are always a great way to inspire friends and family going through trying times. Adding personal advice on what you would do isn't the best idea, seeing as though you are on a personal journey to perfect yourself inside and out. The advice from someone with low self-esteem can differ greatly from the advice of someone without it. What if they take your advice and it proves to be the wrong choice? Giving good advice is easier when you have been through a similar situation and triumphed over it. If you don't know how to be comfortable in your own skin, how can you give advice to a friend experiencing the same thing?

Avoid presenting an opinion that could easily be misinterpreted as a recommendation. When two people are in a negative state, it is hard for them to uplift each other; you must uplift positivity within yourself before you can help others.

5. **Do you find yourself sacrificing your own welfare in order to make that special person in your life happy, whether that person is a friend or a romantic partner?**

A lot of people in the world are so kindhearted that they would give the shirts off their backs. When that type of personality is combined with low self-esteem, the mix can be very dangerous, especially in relationships. A woman with low self-esteem will give away her rent money if it appeases the person she is attempting to court or keep. She might spend money to feel accepted in a crowd or to gain the interest of a person she wishes to be with. Again, as said before, if you suffer from low self-esteem, it is vital to put yourself first. You can't give up your last dime for someone and leave yourself with nothing; even if your life's mission is to help people, you will be no good to them once you've allowed yourself to become too weak to assist anyone.

People find different ways to cope with their personal issues, from eating to shopping. They might try to "drink wine on a beer budget," failing to realize that you cannot disguise your issues with self-indulgence. Some people will spend their entire checks on cars, clothes, and materialistic items—"acting Hollywood," as I call it. Such people spend all their money on toys to make their inner selves feel better, wearing expensive name-brand items to portray to the world that they are wealthy and possess the greatest confidence ever. In reality, they return home to bills on the table, and once all the materialistic items are removed, they're still left with the reality that it's all a facade. Meanwhile, the deeper issues have yet to be touched.

People with low self-esteem become addicted to keeping up this facade to the point of addiction. For example, during this recession, some people still shop five times a week to maintain that habit of fooling the world.

But they can't fool the most important person: themselves. Their spending addiction only adds to problems like depression and isolation.

If you have a spending problem, scale back slowly. Start by taking those five weekly shopping trips down to two or three, easily saving a couple hundred dollars. That money saved could go into investments, bills, or just a nest egg that may come in handy one day. An inner issue like low self-esteem can block one from seeing into the future, much less preparing for that future; meanwhile, masking the issue only makes things more complicated in the long run. We mask our issues in so many ways, making our path ahead even harder because of those choices. Nipping low self-esteem in the bud can reduce those behavioral "side effects" and result in a happier life.

People will go to extreme measures to boost their own self-image. They might surround themselves with those who they feel are lower than them. A skinny girl with self-esteem issues might surround herself with only bigger women as friends or only social outcasts to "shine" among the bunch. Thriving off of others' imperfections is just a bandage covering up the real issue and at some point that bandage will give. Putting a halt to living this facade can help people on the outside realize that the person may need someone to talk to and to open up to about their issues. Some issues are fixable and workable, and others will only get treated with acceptance—the realization that "It'll be what it'll be—nothing more and nothing less."

Everyone knows there's a thin line between love and hate, but there's also a thin line between bringing baggage into a relationship and having your guard up against a normal level of baggage and being too optimistic about finding a future mate with zero baggage. I believe everyone is guilty of bringing baggage into a new relationship: trust issues, past issues, the low self-esteem you gained from a past relationship, drama, and so on. There's nothing worse than trying to fix what someone else caused; after being pushed away, shut out, and put on an emotional roller coaster, a person can only deal with so much before giving up.

When you walk into a new relationship bearing drama from your old relationship, it only slows your progress in putting your past behind you.

Lingering self-esteem issues are part of the reason I advise women to take time to regroup before getting into new relationships. Give those old wounds time to heal, so you can feel renewed and refreshed; relationship on top of relationship can be detrimental to your self-esteem, especially a series of negative relationships.

Once you conquer your self-esteem issues, you may adopt the mentality that you will walk into every new relationship with a clean slate. While you definitely want to think positive, you do not want to walk into every relationship with unrealistic expectations. The new relationship might not work out, and you do not want to you experience the pain of unfulfilled optimism.

You want to walk a thin line—and when I say it's thin, it's thin. You want to build up immunity to the possibility of being hurt, but you also want to give potential mates the benefit of the doubt with a clean slate. You want to make each man (or woman) prove himself and show you he's not going to be like the man prior. Actions speak louder than words, and I believe that saying will always be true. No matter how you say it—"Don't talk about it, be about it" or "Put your money where your mouth is"—you still want to be a woman who holds a man accountable for his behavior.

When you bring certain baggage from past relationships, you risk carrying over paranoia that you developed in your last relationship. This can tremendously affect your new relationship, because healthy relationships require trust and peace of mind. If you suffer from that paranoia, your mind might go on a rampage the first time he doesn't answer his phone, remembering what happened in your last relationship when your ex didn't answer his phone. Just like that, paranoia can cause an argument that could have been easily avoided if you had given him the benefit of the doubt until he gave you a reason to believe otherwise. It may take a while for a woman to find just the right balance, but it is possible. Find what's comfortable for you.

Domestic violence preys on those with low self-esteem—completely submissive women who have lost their ability to stand up for themselves. Domestic violence is about control, and women with low self-esteem they tend to lose some, if not all, of the control they once had over their own lives. Approximately 5.3 million women are abused each year by someone they are romantically involved with, and 1,232 of those women a year will lose their lives.2 We've all seen the *Maury* episodes in which men bring their wives on television to show the world what type of control they have over them, announcing what these women can or cannot do because they are owned by their husbands.

Now, in every relationship, you will have to give up something or change something. For example, some people go to the club every weekend. When they enter a serious, committed relationship, their partner will likely want that to cease. A compromise may be made along the way, but everyone has to alter something to accommodate a relationship. However, completely relinquishing all control over yourself and what you do is a costly mistake. Love is a powerful thing, and when you are in love (or believe at the time that you are in love), those emotions can become addictive.

Love ignites the dopamine system, the system associated with addiction and pleasure.3 This is the same system that causes drug addiction, specifically to the drug known as cocaine. It is vital to thoroughly take your time in selecting the right spouse, because an addictive relationship will lead to obsession and irrational behavior. If you think about it, everyone goes through a rehab phase of sorts after exiting a relationship, experiencing withdrawal from the person that they loved. People will do whatever they can to rid themselves of the toxin: deleting contacts, pictures, and text messages from their phones; destroying or throwing away items associated with memories; blocking or deleting the ex from social networks; and so on.

What started as a natural high becomes a toxin when you begin to lose your appetite, going hours without even realizing you haven't eaten, or becoming sleep-deprived. When your well-being or productivity drops, the situation has become unhealthy for you. Keeping your mind occupied and staying busy can speed the recovery process. Listening to slow songs, lying in bed, and crying will only make matters worse; those constant

---

2   http://www.newchoicesinc.org, as stated by the American Institute on Domestic Violence, although only an approximation.

3   http://www.futurepundit.com, per a study by Dr. Sean Mackey (http://www.futurepundit.com/archives/007579.html).

memories and thoughts can leave you vulnerable to the point of irrational behavior. Naturally, we all may relapse at some point by spying on his Facebook page, calling his phone just to hear his voice, or letting him know in some form or fashion that you miss him. It happens, but only time and your ability to distance yourself completely will help you to move on and get him out of your system.

When you meet someone who possesses many of the qualities you are looking for, and the chemistry is amazing, it is easy to jump in headfirst without giving it much thought. You might enter a relationship quickly, feeling as though you've found the perfect spouse, when in reality everyone puts on his or her interview face in the courting process. When you're wearing your interview face, you have altered your personality to become everything that employer is looking for, trying to ensure that you get that position. The same survival instinct applies to relationships; when a man is attempting to court a woman, he does everything in his power to ensure that he gets that woman. Once a woman gets caught up in his Prince Charming routine of opening car doors and being a complete romantic, she often caves in, whether that means having sex or allowing him the ownership that comes with an official relationship status. Either way, he has won before you have gotten a chance to see the real him.

Eventually, whether someone is wearing an interview face for a job or a relationship, the facade will wear off. Once they get what they want, some men and women become a completely different person. Deciphering whether someone is genuine requires an extended dating process. I suggest waiting at least three or four months before taking it to the next level. If a man is not genuine, his act will eventually fade and he'll become impatience that he has not gotten his prize.

A celebrity once told a friend of mine who is absolutely gorgeous that the reason men of a lower caliber did not seek to court the prettier, self-respecting women out of the crowd is that men know they will have to invest way too much effort. So it is easier to talk to the women who are not so attractive and are wearing little to nothing, because men know without a shadow of a doubt that sleeping with that woman is as good as sold.

If a woman suffering self-esteem issues decides to jump in headfirst instead, the results of that disappointment could be drastic. Not being in a stable state emotionally and getting hurt could cause a woman's condition to worsen.

You also want to steer clear of complicated situations while going through low self-esteem. If he is going through a pending divorce and it has yet to be finalized, or if he has just had a newborn child or still lives with his ex for the "kids' sake," stop! Don't set yourself up for failure. No matter how good of a woman you believe you are, a man in that situation will not let go of his past until he decides to. No matter how much he says you're the better woman, you simply cannot trump some situations. In some cases, you may have the ability to remove him from that previous situation, but by the time you reach that point and finally "win," I am almost sure you will have had to endure so much along the way that you probably will no longer desire the relationship and at times question if it was worth it.

When you compete against another woman, you will dwell on the question, "What does she have that I don't have?" Insecurities may follow.

If it is meant to be, at some point it will be. Rushing it will only confuse things. Patience is a gift from God, and we as women need to utilize it.

Low self-esteem has many side effects, and they aren't printed on a label anywhere. I think if more people were aware of the side effects, they would do more to stay away from this condition that could possibly take control of their lives for God knows how long. When you go through low self-esteem, you are no longer in control of your life. Your self-worth, or lack of it, dictates a lot of your actions and decisions. The most common side effects are depression, weight gain, isolation, promiscuity (excessive sexuality), inability to withstand peer pressure, and suicide. Low self-esteem can lead to horrendous or even deadly outcomes.

Depression: sadness, gloom or dejection; the state of being depressed.

In most cases, depression is the first side effect to set in. Repeatedly thinking negative thoughts about yourself can ignite this condition. It's one thing to think to yourself, "I'm gaining a few pounds." But after you've had that thought a few times, you'll move on to "I'm gaining weight, which means I won't be able to fit in the same sizes as my friends. People will judge me, or men won't approach me." Extreme example, you say? Not at all—many women suffer from these thought patterns.

There are other ways to deal with weight gain besides panicking and overthinking. Purchase identical clothing to the originals and learn how to be okay with your body. If you are still not satisfied with your body, simply start to cut back on what you eat, begin eating healthier foods, and start exercising. Taking baby steps to correct the problem is key; trying to go from eating whatever you want to one day cutting out everything under the sun isn't realistic. I believe that gradually weaning yourself will result in more of a success story.

As humans age, our bodies will age with us, and only proper diet and exercise can keep it close to what it has always been. Where there's a will, there's a way, but the woman in this scenario first has to realize she is starting a downhill spiral over the superficial. A lot of times, people don't say, "I'm gaining weight—I am concerned about my health." The only thing that comes to mind is the materialistic and superficial value of being thin.

Clothing doesn't make the woman—the woman makes the clothing. Instead of overthinking, do what I call "processing and meditation." Weigh all of your options, consider all the facts, and think it through slowly and thoroughly, processing everything. Proper processing helps you avoid making irrational decisions.

Weight gain: a woman's nightmare.

Weight gain is caused by health conditions, nutritional imbalances, or simply eating more than you can burn off. As said before, people often focus on how unattractive weight gain is, but the real issue is your health. We lose 400,000 people a year to obesity,[4] so in some cases, just the slightest possibility of becoming a statistic may be used as motivation to start eating healthy and exercising. Not everyone handles weight gain

---

[4]   http://www.nourishingconnections.com

well, especially if they already had low self-esteem prior to gaining weight. Some find comfort in eating when sad, depressed, or lonely. Some don't eat as much as we think; genetics just do not fall in their favor. Weight gain in a lot of cases is the cause of low self-esteem. The key is learning to control it instead of letting it control you.

Isolation: the complete separation from others; the state of being isolated.

Isolation is another very big side effect of low self-esteem. People who isolate themselves may do so in an attempt to cut down the number of people who will harass them or look at them as an outcast. Learning to distance people in all aspects can lead to a secretive state. Furthermore, isolation acts as a poison, leaving you to face issues on your own and go through life's trials and tribulations with no one by your side. Making decisions in the wrong frame of mind can leave you vulnerable and susceptible to just about anything. When your guard is weak, a person can break it down in no time, especially if you don't have friends and family in your life to look out for your well-being. Isolation also causes you to miss out on adventure and fun activities as you stay confined in your "safe place," whether that place is a room, park, home, or other location. You may feel most comfortable in your safe place away from the general public, but isolation is ultimately self-destructive, because it causes you to miss out on life and go through it alone.

Sexuality: recognition of or emphasis upon sexual matters.

Many gay or bisexual people say they were born the way they are; not everyone believes that's always the case. Some believe that low self-esteem can cause a person to question or act on his or her sexuality. Some people may feel as if they cannot attract the opposite sex for whatever reason and decide to try a same-sex relationship, not because they were born that way but because they feel as if this is their only option. Some teenagers try homosexuality because it is the latest fad, not because that is truly where their heart is.

Questioning your sexuality can also become a spiritual issue, depending on what your beliefs are. Some believe that a higher power will judge a decision to court the same sex. If you're considering a same-sex relationship, your ability to deal with the wrath of those close to you, along with the added judgment of strangers, would have to factor into that decision. Although God is the only person who can pass judgment upon you, it is painful to be judged and criticized by society, whether anyone will admit it aloud or not.

I recently spoke to a teenage girl who would rather stay anonymous. When asked how she felt about her sexuality, she said that she felt like guys in her age group wouldn't give her the time of day because of her weight and her tomboy wardrobe. She had found herself compromising her virginity and performing oral sex only to demoralize herself and be treated inhumanely. Despite being young and despite having previously expressed her desire to feel some sense of being wanted by men, she was now coming to terms with a belief that she was a homosexual woman. She felt as though women may treat her with more understanding and empathy than men. However, I believe it is a preconceived notion that just because a woman may relate strongly to another woman, this eliminates the possibility of mistreatment or heartache. Dating a woman because a man has failed you, or rebounding into a same-sex relationship, can be damaging.

Some women just go through a "curious stage." Acting on this curiosity while dealing with low self-esteem could leave you vulnerable to something foreign to your everyday life—something that might deeply affect you emotionally.

I wanted to briefly touch on those who feel they were born transgendered. I've seen a plethora of television shows featuring many men and women who look as if they were born the opposite of what they really are. It is amazing to witness their transformation and see them finally comfortable in their own skin. Transgendered people suffer extreme cases of low self-esteem stemming from a lack of acceptance. Their emotional turmoil can dissolve once they begin transforming themselves physically. Finally, they can work on what makes them happy, and in time completely conquer their inner issues.

Peer pressure: social pressure by a member of one's peer group to take a certain action, adopt certain values, or otherwise conform in order to be accepted.

Not having the will power to resist peer pressure can be a side effect of low self-esteem. Peer pressure is a powerful force, and it's most predominant in a child's middle-school and high-school years. Adults can experience peer pressure as well; I believe it is just most common in the preteen and teenage community.

Fitting in can feel like a vital goal, but your individuality and unique traits set you apart and are worth celebrating. Some people do things they don't enjoy just to blend in with the crowd they want to be associated with. Others try drugs or alcohol and actually enjoy them, becoming addicted and starting a downward spiral in their lives. These mistakes only worsen the problem; once a woman is addicted to drugs, she might isolate herself from the people who care about her in order to hide her problem.

Those with low self-esteem can become the brunt of the popular kids' jokes. This mockery and lack of acceptance can worsen their isolation, leading to massacres like the Columbine and Virginia Tech shootings. Many innocent lives can be lost when a school is not a safe place for education; people who are teased or bullied become ticking time bombs.

The best way for parents to combat peer pressure is to get involved. Parents should not be afraid to talk to their children and their children's teachers, communicating on any possible signs of bullying, isolation, or abnormal behavior. It truly takes a village to raise a child, and that is something that we as a community should embrace.

Suicide: the intentional taking of one's life.

Suicide is the most serious consequence of low self-esteem; there is no turning back once the deed is done. Suicide is not a side effect; it should be looked at as a drastic final emotional state. Low self-esteem and its side effects can lead up to someone's decision to end his or her life. This decision not only makes a serious statement of how low one is in that point in life, but also makes an even stronger statement of not fearing the one thing that cannot be corrected—of not fearing even the spiritual consequences of such a decision.

Just the thought of not existing causes my palms to sweat, my heart to race, and tears to flow recklessly at the uncertainty of not knowing when my day will come and my fear of what will happen when it does. The idea of knowing when and how one will die and still being able to follow through with the act of suicide leaves me speechless. Spirituality also comes into play regarding what will happen to a person once they perish, and yet many still make the decision to die. In a lot of cases, I believe suicide is a drastic cry for attention—the only way to be heard and to make a statement letting those who were too busy to pay attention to see that you are troubled, at a low point, and in desperate need of love.

Hopefully, an ongoing discussion about self-esteem and how to conquer emotional issues will help someone avoid losing his or her life. It's my belief that everyone has a purpose in life, and if we all put aside the Bible or our theories of what happens after this for a second, we might realize that life is about accomplishing our mission in the present. It may take you years to figure out what your mission is, but I believe it will unveil itself over time.

I also believe low self-esteem and its consequences cause some people to escape to lives of drugs, prostitution, homelessness and so on, leading to a form of suicide in which a person only exists, they no longer live. When people hit rock bottom, I believe, low self-esteem issues have played a role no matter how old they are or what circumstances now surround them.

A lot of self-destructive behavior comes from women attempting to find an outlet—something that helps them escape reality and the state that they are in.

One of the most popular outlets is shopping, and not just among the wealthy. Women find it soothing to shop while they are going through something in life. These women are seeking not to splurge on unnecessary items, but to create a new person. Creating a new look feels like starting over—as if it's a brand new day in a sense. Some women will cut off their hair in search of this sensation as well.

Another popular outlet is food. When you're struggling in life, it's easy to indulge in your favorite cuisine without watching portions or calories.

Although in the moment, eating brings satisfaction, this outlet will only add to your problems, bringing weight gain and health issues into the mix. During a very tough stage in life, it can be hard to think about the future when you've found a temporary fix to your problems.

Other outlets, like crying or moping, can be draining. These two tendencies are more of a hindrance than a help in most situations.

Some outlets can result in positive outcomes; they can keep you active and focused on something other than your current struggles. Exercising and volunteering are good examples of healthy outlets.

Talking out your issues can also be therapeutic. Therapists are so successful because it feels good to talk about your issues and have someone listening and providing supportive, positive feedback rather than judging you. Even if you can't afford a therapist, just talking to a close friend or family member can be soothing. However, people who care for you and your well-being may struggle to detach themselves from your personal situations. For example, if you reveal to a friend that you caught your husband cheating, it would be hard for that friend to avoid judging the husband the next time they cross paths. It is usually best to have a stranger evaluate the situation because of the lack of emotional attachment to both parties.

When you reveal your personal business to someone close to you, and at some point an altercation with that person arises, that sacred information can be used as blackmail or as leverage to make you feel low. Often, this tactic works, and the betrayal on top of the loss of a friend becomes overwhelming. Naturally, you're not supposed to let your opponent see you sweat, but when the adrenaline and anger subside, the hurt and betrayal remains.

Outlets are simply a means for escape, if only for a minute. Some outlets are good for you; others only make matters worse. The promise of momentary escape can make dangerous outlets "worth the risk" to some, with drugs and alcohol being the top two that offer that temporary fix. The consequences of alcoholism and drug addiction can be quite severe, especially if the combination is combined. If you find yourself attempting to conquer addiction, you'll need every ounce of your inner strength to prevail.

I have one piece of blunt, straight-to-the-point advice: Don't let your past affect your future.

Reacting to baggage from the past can prompt you to make mistakes that affect your future. The best thing to do when you encounter low self-esteem issues or problems that may start a downward spiral is to confront the issue. Allowing the problem to linger and fester will only hinder your growth process—and, in some cases, give you a defensive and negative outlook on life. In my personal experience, the fear of being alone ignited my self-esteem issues.

I realized I had low self-esteem when I noticed my tendency to allow men to walk over me as if my value were nonexistent. No matter how beautiful I was told I was or how many people tried to date me, I didn't hold much regard for myself or think I was worth much. Having low self-esteem while wanting and looking for love is a destructive combination.

I believe my emotional issues began when I had my first child at sixteen and had to endure the pregnancy without support from my child's father. Adopting a phobia of being alone, I lost my voice that year and became tolerant of unacceptable behavior. Just to avoid being alone, I began going above and beyond for the men I got in relationships with. I dished out money, offered undeserved praise, and did whatever I could to keep them in a relationship with me, no matter how badly I was treated or how often I was cheated on.

My strategy of being this ride-or-die chick backfired. Men didn't cherish me because I was a good woman; greed consumed them, and they demanded more money and more materialistic items. I felt as if I had no choice but to continue what I had started, handing over my rent money at times just to hear "I love you" and to capture a few moments of their time. By the time I tried to put a halt to the monster I had created, it was too late; instead of getting affectionate words or quality time, I got verbal abuse instead—so much of it that I broke down. I no longer had confidence; I was insecure and couldn't risk getting replaced and being alone. Once men realized how much I was willing to endure to avoid being alone, I pretty much had dug my own grave.

What started out as a phobia had turned into something much worse: I had developed low self-esteem, which in turn cost me my confidence and put me into a depression. I began to feel as if I wasn't worth anything; I lost all inner positivity. I made reckless decisions while in such a low state. However, I learned that the key to conquering my issues was going back to the root of the problem and working from there. I knew I had to conquer the fear of being alone before I could get rid of my other issues. Running from my fears only made matters worse, and I needed to confront and learn from my issues. What didn't kill me would most definitely make me stronger.

An issue I share with many other women in America is that of being too independent or too dominant. Over independence can put your relationship in a deficit. By requiring no assistance and having the mentality of "I can do it by myself," the woman handicaps the man by not requiring him to do much. Normally, women are the ones who put the most energy into relationships, especially in the beginning. When you bring a lot to the table, are very attentive to your partner's needs and wants, initiate most of the communication, and do the majority of the finances without requiring or asking for help, you have unintentionally handicapped your man.

In other cases, some men might not naturally be willing to put up a fight for you. For example, when you're upset and walk off, don't be appalled when he doesn't chase after you, trying to work things out. When you dominate a relationship and put in more than you're getting out, it's easy for a man's personal traits to go undetected. Men are naturally hunters, and if you are too dominant or independent, you strip them of what is supposed to come naturally. Women will put the blame on themselves when a man doesn't run after them or fight for the relationship, telling themselves, "He doesn't want me," and deciding there is something wrong with them. In this way, very strong women can easily suffer low self-esteem. In reality, no matter how good of a woman you are or how much you bring to the table, he is who he is, and not even you being a good woman can change that. You cannot change anyone else; until you realize that, you leave yourself susceptible to being hurt and turning all the negative energy on yourself.

As stated before, using money to appease the other party will only last for so long if she has only adopted the habit in an attempt to please and that is not naturally who she is. However, when a woman is truly naturally a person who caters to her relationship both financially and emotionally, as I am, she can easily be taken advantage of. So, in some cases, women can't be themselves in fear of their natural kindness being observed as a weakness. Each case is different, and I am not sure I can advise anyone to change who they are, holding themselves back just to match the lesser energy of a partner or spouse. Such a forced change might be more harmful than helpful to the person's relationship. Every situation is different, and every woman should process her situation and weigh her options with a lot of thought.

"Forget about today's standard of only satisfying men. Satisfy me emotionally, fulfill me intellectually, love me unconditionally, respect me wholeheartedly, support me indefinitely, encourage me spiritually, and then you may indulge in my curves. If it's too much work, then you're not man enough for me. Go pick the apples closest to the ground—but trust me, the better tasting ones are at the top."—Unknown

Some people make decisions based on a perceived lack of love at home. Certain personalities can be more aloof than others, wanting space or time alone, but everyone cries out for some type of attention and wants love to be shown in some form or fashion: support for their endeavors, verbal affection, physical gestures, and so on. Furthermore, to be shunned, disowned, mistreated, or neglected by anyone you deem close to you, especially your parents, can be devastating and can give rise to a plethora of problems, from behavioral issues to isolation. Only time will tell how such a child will grow up, and the answer depends on whether the person recovers as he or she grows, or instead drags out childhood issues.

A lot of people who endure sexual abuse as children grow up to let those issues manifest in and affect their adult lives. Molestation is a traumatic experience, and a good number of people never recover. Many murderers and pedophiles were abused themselves in their childhood or teenage years, and then became abusers themselves, continuing an ongoing cycle. Embedding negative things into a child's vulnerable mind can cause low self-esteem at an early age; parents must be as active in these children's lives as possible.

Many parents seem to overlook that everything and anything that a child experiences, witnesses, or encounters in some way can easily sculpt the person they will grow to be. The new trend seems to be fatherless children; more and more children are raised by single mothers. Growing up without a mother, or without a father, will surely affect a person at some point—whether for better or worse, time will tell. Regardless, it is important for us as parents to understand the seriousness of the absence of the other parent and how that affects our children's development. Some children develop low self-esteem from feeling abandoned by the absent parent. They might ask themselves whether they were left behind because of something they did. They might feel saddened by the lack of a mother to confide in or a father to give them away at their wedding.

Rebellion is a form of communication for youth. The action doesn't have to be extreme—it can be a simple gesture of lashing out. Unfortunately, some kids will act out with drugs, severely violent behavior, or frivolous sexuality. When teens hit the rebellious stage, low self-esteem can drive them to horrible destinations.

Whether you live near Denver's Colfax or Atlanta's Fulton Industrial, prostitution is no stranger to our streets; this is what many rebellious women have ultimately resorted to. Several times, I've spoken with a woman who went to prison for drugs and prostitution, and she called prostitution an addiction. In a recent phone interview, she said that prostitution helped her low self-esteem issues, because it made her feel wanted. She felt that men came to her because of attraction and that prostitution would boost her self-esteem.

"The feeling of being wanted and feeling beautiful made me become an addict and yearn for that attention that I wasn't getting," she said. Low self-esteem caused her to run to prostitution, which led her to drugs as an escape. She wound up in prison, leaving four children behind in the system to fend for themselves. She could only pray that she hadn't started a generational curse.

I believe prostitution will eventually worsen one's psychological state. Interacting with men or women who could care less about your well-being violates what's supposed to be something sacred between two people. To have sex without getting meaning out of it is to not know your worth. Something I learned long ago is the power of the vagina. Many women do not understand this power and frivolously have casual sex in order to feel loved or desired, but regret usually sets in at some point. Some women find themselves becoming nymphomaniacs just to feel desirable and wanted for that short period of time. Now, of course, as we all know, there are rules that the streets go by. If a woman sleeps with a large number of men, she is a slut or whore, but if a man does it, he gets praise for the head count. We live in a world consumed with double standards; it's just the way things are, and it's an unfair judgment, although I do not agree with promiscuous behavior. Once you make a name for yourself as a promiscuous woman, it is hard to rid yourself of the reputation. The rumors and verbal taunting only add to self-esteem issues. Trying to fix how you feel about yourself with sexual intercourse will result in an inner catastrophe, in my opinion; it's a temporary fix at best. Promiscuous behavior will not make your problems go away or make you feel loved; it will only make matters worse.

Not far from that subject is pregnancy—specifically, teen pregnancy, an issue way too many teens are becoming familiar with. I myself was one of the many teenage girls who got pregnant at a young age. A lot of girls, and in some cases guys, want to have kids in order to fill an empty void. They see their future children as someone they can love who will love them back. Teenage pregnancy can be a cry for attention.

So many obstacles and trials could be avoided if we just spoke up about our inner suffering instead of acting on it in potentially unhealthy ways. Having a child at a young age is such a life-altering decision that only when you hear the cries of a baby and realize it belongs to you does it hit that you have bitten off far more than you can chew. Parenthood either makes or breaks teens, and if it breaks them, they'll stray away from responsibility. Abandoning a child will surely affect that child in some way, possibly igniting an ongoing cycle of low self-esteem.

We have to finally put a halt to the saga by raising our children in a more efficient way, without bringing any of our baggage into raising our children. We can't let our issues stop us from doing the right thing the second time around. Just because you didn't have health insurance or your mother never gave you a bedtime, that doesn't mean you have to keep up unhealthy traditions.

Putting a child to sleep at a decent time, for example, is very critical, especially while the child is in school. It is said that breakfast is the fuel needed to help a child function correctly, but breakfast won't do much good if he or she hasn't received a proper night's rest. Eight hours of sleep is the suggested amount of time we all have been told we need for our bodies to properly rest, but for children ranging from toddlers to middle-schoolers, it is said that ten to twelve hours of rest a day is ideal, factoring naps in the equation as well.[5] Some parents might consider this excessive, but we want to at least make sure our children are getting eight hours. This helps both the child and the parent: the child gets necessary rest, and the parent gets a little rest and relaxation time as well.

Other parenting considerations, like making your child dentist appointments every six months, along with doctor's appointments and regular visits to the eye doctor, are important and should be done more in our community. The objective is to stop the different generational curses and unhealthy habits and strive to become a better person within, for ourselves and our children.

While one is working on breaking unhealthy cycles, it is important to break the welfare cycle as well.

Welfare: financial or other assistance to an individual or family from a city, state, or national government.

The key word in that definition is *assistance*. Welfare is designed as a supplement for hard times, not income to live off of indefinitely. Overdependence on welfare doesn't happen to a specific age group; recipients range from teenage mothers to women well in their adult lives.

---

[5] http://www.webmd.com

This source of supposedly free money, free food, and a cheap place to live seems like a gold mine to many; too many women become comfortable in the welfare system. These women learn to be content living off a set amount, not desiring more out of life.

Some maintain the facade "balling" by creating the perception that they have worked hard for the things they possess. They become addicted to the attention they get for such a status. However, if the reputation was stripped away and they had nothing but a few materialistic items, would that be enough to motivate them? I've personally watched an older woman spend the majority of her life dependent on welfare, and when her children came of age, they were also content to be welfare dependent. I believe low self-esteem is partially to blame in a lot of these cases. It is important to push each other toward greatness and to break the cycle of women that have become very lethargic and would rather sit at home doing nothing than work and achieve more in life.

It is very easy to get caught up in the system. By all means, if it's needed, use the resources available to you. But avoid abusing the system. Strive for more in life. Receive a hand up, not just a handout.

There is also the possibility of getting caught up in a completely different kind of system: jail.

I believe that our black men have the hardest time staying out of the jail system, compared to other ethnicities. A study published by the Bureau of Justice Statistics showed that 4,777 per 100,000 black men were in jail, compared to only 727 white men per 100,000 and only 1,760 Latinos per 100,000. This is a self-help book for women—I bet you're wondering what the percentage of men going to jail has to do with us. African American women are losing not only our black men, but our men, period, to the system. It has everything to do with us, making the ratio of women per man ridiculous in certain states. The struggle to find and keep a mate against those odds can contribute to low self-esteem.

I cannot speak on the males' behalf, but I believe that the majority of women in jail possess low self-esteem. Such an issue can easily put a woman in a vulnerable state, making her feel jealousy, envy, rage, and so on. Of course, not every woman sentenced to jail time has low self-esteem, but by the time the whole procedure is finished, low self-esteem will claim a few prisoners. Inmates become accustomed to the conditions of jail, getting free meals, a roof over their heads, and discipline. So when they are released back into society, they have a hard time adjusting. They are still not free; they must deal with probation, parole, halfway homes, house arrest, a variety of classes, and so on. They may find themselves getting sucked into the system again, unable to stay out of it, whether they suffer an inability to adjust to real life, beat bad habits, or cope with the state of being halfway free. Confronting your inner issues could possibly keep you from having to experience that life-altering road.

Drugs and alcohol can contribute to existing issues and create that downward affect. These outlets offer supposed escape while in reality letting your problems fester, eating away at your insides. Nothing good can come out of holding something in; you just end up making yourself sick internally. You can only escape your problems for so long, and the more drugs you consume, the more you risk ending your problems permanently by overdose or another accident, not to mention putting yourself at risk for different viruses by sharing needles. Low self-esteem should be taken seriously, because it can send you down paths that leave your life in a complete catastrophe.

Thus far I've addressed low self-esteem issues in teenagers and younger women, but self-esteem problems can follow you through all stages of life. Many women who are married with careers and are enjoying their so-called prime also suffer from this disease. I believe that just like the chicken pox, low self-esteem can be worse when it strikes in adulthood. Aging, a midlife crisis, the past, weight gain, an unhealthy marriage, health issues, or just issues that affect a woman physically can serve as triggers for low self-esteem.

Aging: advanced years; old age.

All women will begin to show signs of aging at some point, whether their skin begins to wrinkle or their breasts begin to lose their form. No woman is exempt from having to face the fact that they are getting older. Some women refuse to accept this reality and get cosmetic surgery to restore what they once saw as perfection.

Drinking, drug use, sun exposure, and a lot of other factors can add to how quickly a person ages. Just like death, this is a phase of life that you cannot cheat; however, some have managed to impede the process. With the proper diet and exercise, experts like Jack LaLanne and fitness instructor Richard Simmons have become victorious at slowing the aging process. Even in their nineties and sixties, respectively, they look amazing, not to mention healthy. If you don't become proactive about taking care of yourself, your body will begin to deteriorate after years of everyday wear and tear.

Midlife crisis: a period of psychological stress occurring in middle age, thought to be triggered by a physical, occupational, or domestic event, such as menopause, diminution of physical prowess, job loss, or departure of children from the home.

I'm sure everyone knows someone who has gone through a midlife crisis, male or female, family member or friend. Such crises are very common for those in middle age. Men are more culturally notorious for them, as many wives were left for a younger woman or finding a sports car in their garages out of the blue. However, women aren't exempt from extreme irrational behavior, and in some cases, low self-esteem can be the cause of their actions.

When women no longer feel good about themselves, they sometimes choose to break out of their normal routine and do something to spice themselves up again, to feel alive. I call it the paprika stage—out of nowhere, a kick of spice jumps in and livens up what may have become a dull life.

I've seen both males and females resort to dating much younger people. Whether it's just the thrill of having something new or the ego boost of attracting someone younger, I'm not sure. During this stage, a lot of money is frivolously spent, possibly causing the accumulation of debt. The midlife crisis can be dangerous stage, because people who have never taken a risk in their lives suddenly become rambunctious, making very risky decisions. These decisions can bring down what took years to build, leaving many wondering, "What have I done?"

The reality of getting older may be too much for some to bare, but the harsh reality is that we are only guaranteed one thing: death. In my eyes, it's a blessing to make it to middle age. Many will never get the opportunity to reach that stage of life; embrace it.

The past: a stage no one can ever forget.

We've all let issues from our past shape the future, whether we've brought baggage into a romantic relationship or allowed our bad experiences to change us. A lot of people who experience sexual abuse, abandonment, or other traumatic experiences never really recover, dragging their issues along with them as they get older. I let the taunting and teasing when I was younger sculpt my character, growing a tough exterior when really I was a totally different person on the inside. I pushed people away, gave off a nonchalant attitude, and voluntarily became a loner. By the time I was twenty, it was already hard to change; I can only imagine how hard such changes are in middle age. The older we get, the harder it will become to finally face our past and say, "I will not allow my past to affect my future."

Time may heal all, but allowing too much of it to pass before facing your issues can have the opposite effect of hindering progress. Turning back the hands of time isn't an option, and at some point any lingering issues have to be addressed.

I interviewed a woman in her fifties who chose to remain anonymous. She stated that being sexually abused by her father as a child, being dark skinned, feeling invisible, and enduring a verbally and physically abusive relationship caused her self-esteem to plummet and also caused her to rebel against the male species. She reached a point where her body rejected being penetrated, and she turned to masculine women, trying to deceive her mind by visually seeing a man but sexually not having to be penetrated.

When the body gets to a point where it rejects penetration, this is called vaginismus.

Vaginismus: vaginal tightness causing discomfort, burning, pain, penetration problems, or complete inability to have intercourse.

When someone experiences a trauma that affects them sexually, even after successfully having intercourse, this is specifically called secondary vaginismus.

The woman I interviewed had found herself in a stage where she was confused about her faith, her sexuality, and her future. Plenty of women can relate to this story—unfortunately, our pasts at times affects all of us at one time or another.

Weight Gain

Weight gain is something the majority of us are all too familiar with. Some women purposely gain weight, and others have metabolisms that are too slow to burn off their intake. Many obstacles can contribute to weight gain, from pregnancy to the slowing of the metabolism with age. Menopause plays a large factor in weight gain due to hormonal changes. Pregnancy is the most common source of weight gain for women of all ages, because our bodies undergo a transformation.

It seems safe to say that majority of mothers gain during pregnancy and losing that weight as a new mother can be strenuous, involving issues one has never had to deal with before. Staying focused and encouraged is hard to do while juggling your everyday parenting routine. It is very easy to get discouraged and slip into a depression, opening up the door to low self-esteem. When women lose their hourglass figures, they can feel as if they've lost their sexy essence, which is a lot to accept, especially for those women who are very sexual and in tune with their bodies. Some women never recover from childbirth and completely let themselves go physically; once at an older age, they find out that low self-esteem isn't just for the young.

Weight gain isn't all about physical appearances. Older women who become overweight are screaming out to become a health statistic. One of the girls I interviewed during the making of this book lost her mother to obesity. Weight gain can cost you more than your self-esteem; it can cost you your life.

Unhealthy Marriage

Unhealthy: not in a state of good or normal health; in an unsound, weak, or morbid condition.

I don't know about you, but I prefer to stay away from anything that could be defined as unhealthy, especially when it comes to marriage. Marriage is supposed to be harmonious, offering up some of the best moments and years of your life. If you've heard it once, you've heard it a thousand times: "Marriage isn't what it used to be" and "You can get them, but can you keep them?" I think everybody at some point is guilty of becoming a little too comfortable in a relationship, whether only for a little while or indefinitely. That comfort zone can easily turn into a danger zone.

My mother has always told me, "How the relationship starts out is how it is expected to be," and I could not agree with her more. I believe both parties should always keep the mentality that they're competing for their spouse; this courting mentality keeps the relationship fresh, exciting, and new. This is important, because everyone is replaceable. The initial stages of dating involve a lot of spontaneity, romance, and adventure. In the beginning, everything may be marvelous sexually, financially, physically, and romantically. But as time passes and that relationship turns into marriage, some of those qualities begin to fade. A woman may decide that she "has" her man, or vise versa, and feel no need to go the extra mile. Trying to impress a spouse can start to seem unnecessary. In actuality, working to keep your spouse satisfied and happy is imperative to a marriage, and both parties should possess this goal.

What you won't do, another person will, whether that something is cooking or sex. If you fail to play your role, your spouse might stray and find someone who will do the things you once did. I believe no matter what your title is—girlfriend, fiancée, or wife—that both parties should bring their A game, never slacking in any duty that another person could potentially fulfill.

Now, as a woman ages, her body will go through phases; however, that does not mean her attraction has to fade. The objective is to shed the stereotype that just because a woman is older, she is obligated to wear panties three times her size, go to bed with a head full of rollers, and lose the sex drive that she once had. Physical attraction plays a huge role in relationships. Now, I'm not saying a woman should be the same size and wear the same things she did eight years prior, but going from a size five to a size eighteen or going from wearing form-fitting clothes to grandma clothing is drastic. If your spouse loves you for who you are, not even gaining weight can change that, but you put your relationship at risk by becoming unappealing to your man, leaving open the option for him to stray to infidelity.

Keep the lingerie in stock, offer cards that say "I Love You," make it clear that you value who he is as a man just because, and initiate sex on a regular basis, not just birthdays and holidays. It is so important to keep that flame lit and to continue to stay desirable to your man.

Men should follow this advice as well. If a man with an LL Cool J physique attracts a woman, and she considers that her type, is she expected to later find his new Heavy D build just as attractive, just because she loves him? The answer is no. I believe that we cannot necessarily help what we're attracted to or change what ignites our libido.

When the truth is revealed about how a man may have begun to feel less attracted to his wife, she might develop low self-esteem. The ensuing argument could even cause verbal and physical abuse to arise. Lacking confidence, on top of lacking an interested or supportive spouse, can cause a downward spiral of self-esteem. Financial independence can build your self-esteem as opposed to knocking it down. Being able to get up and buy that outfit that makes you feel like a million bucks is important. When you become completely dependent, and the relationship for whatever reason begins to go sour, you'll find yourself feeling inferior, rather than equal. It can make you feel low to have to go to the man who should be your equal and ask for money, explaining what you plan to use it on as if you are a child. Complete dependence is unhealthy and can be detrimental to your self-esteem.

LESSON THREE

HEALTH AND PHYSICAL ISSUES

Many women have to fight for every day of their lives because of unavoidable medical or psychological issues. Some issues that arise aren't life threatening, just life altering, and some may just alter you physically without causing harm. Varicose veins, menopause, breast cancer, other types of cancers and chemotherapy are all just examples of the many different issues a woman may have to face at some point in her life.

The importance of hair is instilled in women at a young age, with childhood rivalries breaking out over who has the "good hair." Women use extensions, wigs, and ready-made ponytails to bring style and variety to the table. So when a woman has to endure a traumatic experience like chemotherapy and lose all of her hair, or undergo a mastectomy, which is the removal of the breast, it is easy for a woman to develop low self-esteem. When a woman loses a trait that helped define her femininity, it can take a lot of soul searching to overcome those inner issues and reach acceptance of her new physical form.

Low self-esteem can lead to dangerous health issues and side effects. Some of the more serious cases of low self-esteem may require outside help. Issues like obsessive-compulsive disorder (OCD), anorexia, bulimia, and phobias are some of the more serious consequences that may not be easy to defeat alone.

OCD: obsessive-compulsive disorder.-is an anxiety disorder in which people have unwanted and repeated thoughts, feelings, ideas, sensations (obsessions), or behaviors that make them feel driven to do something (compulsions)

OCD is something that I personally suffered from. I think of it as both a blessing and a curse, because I don't know whether I'd be the same person without it, but OCD can hinder a person's life. OCD can play a big role in the issues that a lot of women have in relationships. Some women overanalyze so much that they fall into obsession, which can result in a drastic reaction when change takes place. For example, if a woman with OCD is accustomed to her spouse calling every morning and talking to her several times throughout the day, she might have a mental issue if she suddenly doesn't hear from him one morning. The reason behind her husband's silence could be completely innocent, but OCD can take complete control of the mind. By the time a line of communication is opened up, a person with OCD may have come up with ninety different reasons he didn't call, hyping it up to the point of internal fury. A woman might act on these emotions without even confirming what had actually occurred. By the time she converses with him and hears his excuses, she may have already developed trust issues over what could've been nothing. Had he stuck to the normal routine, she wouldn't have had an issue, but unusual situations arise now and again, and not everything can always be routine. He might be late to work because of the weather, or his cell phone may not be getting reception where he is.

What is naturally supposed to be a woman's intuition can be easily overridden by confusion. I'm sometimes unsure whether to trust my own instincts, as it might be the OCD talking. If he really is cheating or doing something wrong, this will eventually be exposed; as the old saying goes, "What's done in the dark always comes to light." Jumping the gun and pushing people away only increases the chances of being alone, isolated, and depressed. OCD is a serious disease, and in my opinion, a form of torture, because you can't control your thoughts; there is no escaping your own mind. Paranoia, anxiety, and repetitive thoughts can in time break down the best of us.

As hopeless as OCD can make you feel, conquering it is worth the effort and time. Through persistence, not to mention a lot of trial and error, you can become healthy again. A study published by the National Institute of National Health shows that 2.2 million American adults encounter OCD in a given year. Forty million will undergo some sort of anxiety disorder, OCD included.6

Phobia: a persistent, irrational fear of a specific object, activity or situation that leads to a compelling desire to avoid.

Sometimes, bad things come in pairs, and phobias can come with low self-esteem. These fears range from being scared of clowns to feeling terrified of the sounds people make; each phobia is horrifying in its own little way. I don't believe that phobias are connected directly to low self-esteem, but to the issues causing the low self-esteem. Such fears can block prosperity and a personal growth and needs to be brought under control. Phobias truly dominate some people's issues, and they must face their fears.

Some phobias cannot be conquered, but they can be accepted. For example, when a woman's low self-esteem has led her to depression and then to the fear of death, there's no way to control that phobia. The only thing she can do is grow to respect and embrace the aging process, accepting that she doesn't have control over everything.

Certain phobias that will be harder to defeat than others, but time, dedication, and determination can prevail.

Anorexia nervosa—is an eating disorder that makes people lose more weight than is considered healthyfor their age and height

Anorexia nervosa is a huge problem in our teenage community. The propaganda for being thin is in full effect—on television, in magazine ads, you name it—giving off the illusion that the prettiest women are skinny, small, or petite. The majority of the latest and hottest fashions are only available in certain sizes, and many boys in high school will only be seen with a girl whom society as deemed suitable. The pressure to be accepted can cause young girls to undergo this physical issue.

---

6   http://www.nimh.nih.gov

Of course, anorexia can affect adults as well, sometimes leaving them unable to take care of their responsibilities due to illness. Anorexia can cause severe health issues like osteoporosis, cardiac arrest, and liver and kidney damage. The lack of vitamins can affect the hair, nails, and skin as well. Anorexia is sometimes even deadly; the body can only be deprived of nutrients for so long. Low self-esteem can be a direct cause of anorexia.

This disease is curable; the key is to get to a comfortable size in a healthy way. It is possible to become the size you desire by exercising and sticking to a healthy diet.

Bulimia: also called binge-purge syndrome, a habitual disturbance mostly affecting young women of normal weight, characterized by frequent episodes of grossly excessive food intake followed by self-induced vomiting to avert weight gain.

A lot of people associate bulimia and anorexia as nearly the same thing. In my opinion, they share no similarities beyond the fact that they are both disorders. Those who are bulimic can disguise their illness much more easily than those going through anorexia. They may be a normal size for their age and height, with their issues going weeks, months, or sometimes even years without being detected.

Oral trauma, gastric reflux, cardiac arrest, and dehydration are only a few dangers associated with Bulimia. Low self-esteem and the desire to be perceived a certain way combined are fuel to this wildfire. Is avoiding weight gain worth the possibility of compromising your life? Eventually, the health of a bulimic woman will deteriorate until she is unable to be her best anymore. Doesn't that defeat the purpose? There are healthier ways to deal with peer pressure.

Most people tend to dance to the beat of the same drum. Only the confident women who are comfortable with themselves can be trendsetters who urge others to break the cycle and dance to their own beat. However, before worrying about setting trends with your outward appearance, you have to master yourself within.

The role of our minds in our well-being goes undetected; people don't really recognize its importance. *The Secret* by Rhonda Byrne is a study guide that will educate you in depth on how the Law of Attraction works. Her theory is simple: you will get back the energy you put out with your thoughts, words, and actions. Eventually, your visions, thoughts, and feelings will at some point manifest into reality. In other words, it's vital that you think positive and try to be positive. This is kind of like the concept of soul food—said to have been named because of the time, love, and positive energy that's put into the preparation of the meal to make it taste the way it does.

Some will not eat at fast-food restaurants because they feel that there's negative energy within the food, because those preparing the meals aren't putting their souls into it. The food wasn't made with love, so by consuming it, they would be putting negative energy in their bodies. This is only one example out of many that a person trying to abide by the Law of Attraction would go by.

Being in a negative state brings negative emotions. Even if you feel that the Law of Attraction is fictional, what could you lose by giving it a try?

Low self-esteem and its consequences can hinder you from making a name for yourself. Many women waste time doubting their craft, isolating themselves, and thinking negative when they should be out there networking and making a name for themselves, with positive comments and feedback assuring them that they are on a great path. As I said before, the ultimate goal is to get to a point where you do not need validation from others; self-gratification is all you should need.

You also want to get to a point where you can forgive everything and everybody that ever caused you any harm. You have to completely cleanse yourself of any potentially toxic emotion; nothing good will come from letting your past fester. Give these feelings to a higher power to deal with, for the battle isn't yours—it's the Lord's.

"Forgive, but never forget" is a wise saying. If you forgive and choose to forget as well, you leave yourself vulnerable to making the same mistake again. If you make the same mistake twice, who else can you blame but yourself? At that point, you just have to take it as a lessoned learned and move on. For those who have a hard time with this step, my personal advice is to tap into your spirituality. Now, I'm not saying who you should believe in or how you should go about seeking that personal relationship, but when you need someone to turn, to there is no one better than your God.

Faith and believing are like first cousins. Belief is exactly what is left in the pot once faith is boiled down. If you are a nonbeliever, what would you lose by believing? Would you rather believe something that turns out to be false, or not believe something that turns out to be true?

With my eyes closed and head bowed, I will say a prayer for every woman about to embark on this journey.

They say to give up is a sign that you no longer care, but I say it's just you realizing that you deserve better or simply just more.

LESSON FOUR

CHANGING FOR THE BETTER

To improve your self-esteem, it is important to get to the root of the problem, acknowledging where the issues lie and mapping out a plan for healing yourself.

As stated before, I believe the majority of low self-esteem issues arise from physical issues, and you have to decide whether your less desirable physical traits are something you're willing to live with or need to be fixed. If you have issues with your eye color, you can wear contacts—there's even a surgery that you can undergo. For hair that won't grow past a certain length, you can wear extensions—or, if you want longer eyelashes, you can buy them at your local beauty supply. However, some physical features can only be altered with a cosmetic procedure, and you have to decide whether you're financially and emotionally willing to go that far just to get a step closer to what you would consider perfection.

I believe that we were made specifically as we are for a reason; however, we only get one life, and we were made to take risks and live life to the fullest. Whatever your decision, you have to say to yourself, "This is where my self-esteem problem originates from, and this is the path I need to go down to fix it." Nothing worth having will be easy; you will have to make many sacrifices along the way to the outcome that you desire. But the reward of feeling happy and complete within is worth the sweat and tears of the roller-coaster journey.

Once you have formed a plan, the next step is to surround yourself with positive people. Many Americans are still friends with people they went to school with or grew up with in general. It's great to have held on to friendships and kept open that door of communication, but if you have outgrown anyone, let them go! Just because you've kept contact or have known a person for a long period of time does not mean they are on the same page as you in life. So if they possess an "I'm content with flipping burgers" attitude when you approach them with your dreams and aspirations to be a lawyer or doctor, you will get a lot of negative feedback that will eventually, if not immediately, bring you down.

Negative energy and negative people can quickly disintegrate your positivity. Birds of a feather flock together, as they say, so associate yourself with people and things you admire and respect. I doubt very seriously that a group of millionaires would sit around conversing with someone who didn't care about financial success. People come into your life for a season or a reason, and it's up to you to figure out the purpose of those in your life. This goes for family members as well, if they tease you about your weight or whatever else you have insecurities with. You have control; run your relationships how you see fit. Strangers, of course, are out of your jurisdiction, but even then, you can at least walk away when someone has offended you. The point is, you do not have to subject yourself to negativity any longer; it's your turn to take control of your destiny.

If we put as much energy into ourselves and our own dreams as we do supporting and believing in others, we'd be one step closer to success.

Once you've determined who should and shouldn't be in your life, you now have to adjust the ones that are worth keeping. Relationships are often one-sided, and you never reap any benefit from them, even if that person is a positive person. In any relationship, whether it is a friendship or romantic relationship, people become accustomed to a dynamic, even if it's not an even dynamic. We often support the goals and aspirations of others as opposed to our own, putting our personal need for support on the back burner. A healthy relationship will nourish your dreams as well. As the old saying goes, a closed mouth doesn't get fed; when your need for support goes unannounced, and you yourself become content with the way the relationship is, nothing will ever be done about the issue.

I believe this issue of inequality is the most common issue in romantic relationships; this is where I personally always fell short. I gave so much in my relationships that I didn't require men to do much for me. By lowering your standards in this way, you wind up with a new breed of dependent man who wants the woman to be the provider. Also, trying so hard in a relationship may send off the wrong signals, causing your kindness to be mistaken for a weakness.

There is such a thing as loving someone too much. You may find yourself constantly thinking about him (or her), texting him and wanting to monopolize his time. But in the midst of all that, your productivity rate drops tremendously. You become more focused on loving—and loving hard if you will—than focusing on the things you have to get done and putting that energy into accomplishing your goals. Women tend to lose themselves in relationships by giving their all but neglecting themselves and their aspirations in the process. When you address the issue, a man will make the necessary changes if he cares about your feelings.

My mother always told me that only two things will make a person change: pain or pleasure. If a man cannot accommodate your concerns and give you the support you need, I believe his so-called love for you was never genuine. If someone told him he could have a million dollars for making those exact changes, those changes would be made without a doubt, because he would be making them for something he desires. If he would be willing to go the extra mile for money, why not do the same thing for you? Slowly but surely, you will find out who has *your* best interests at heart.

The days of the one-sided relationships have to come to a screeching halt. You must focus on your health, well-being, and goals, leaving the relationship in a perfect balance, with enough love and affection for your spouse as well as enough time and energy for yourself. Losing someone you love if he is not willing to make the necessary changes can be one of the hardest things you'll have to do, but remember, you're worth it.

Time heals everything. Space allows your thoughts to process and good-byes only opens the door for another's hello.

The root of your self-esteem problems can ignite more and more issues. At times, these issues can be hard to identify through your clouded judgment. By making a diagram, you can visually see your issues and where you need to start. From there, you'll slowly but surely eliminate these issues, one by one. Below is my personal diagram; you'll be able to see how easily it created my downward spiral.

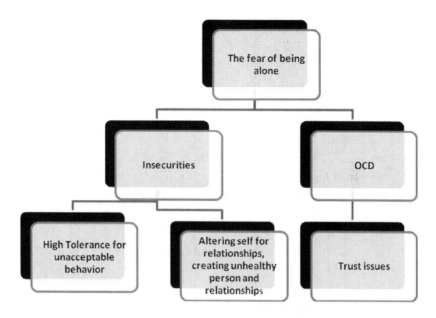

Just that easily, my fear of being alone caused so many other issues. If I would've addressed my fear in its beginning stages, the rest may have been prevented. Visually being able to pinpoint the troubled areas helped me go back and make the necessary steps to a road of recovery.

When you make your diagram, start working with the root of the issue. With time, effort, and a lot of work, all can be corrected. Those of you whose issues are entirely emotional will have an easier time than someone who's dealing with the physical side. If your issues are physical, even a diagram will leave you with only so many options on how to solve them. You can adapt to love your physical traits, get a cosmetic procedure done, stay in a negative state, or, in the case of a weight or fitness issue, slowly but surely make the physical change needed. Losing weight is hard; it requires determination, willpower, and the ability to change habits. Along the way, it is very easy for someone to become discouraged and encounter setbacks.

If you want cosmetic surgery, making this happen might be difficult as well. It can take a while to raise the money for those expensive procedures. After making your diagram, it might be best to keep up your motivation with a few strategies.

For example,

- Put up positive sticky notes in your favorite rooms in the house
- Buy the bra or dress size you desire to fit into and look at it every day
- Set a goal you want to meet, along with the date you want to meet it, and do a calendar countdown
- Mark off days until surgery
- Draw a thermostat and fill it in every time you accumulate more money, in order to gain a visual of how far you've come and how far you still have to go
- Start pampering yourself in preparation for a new you, symbolizing a new beginning

Hopefully some, if not all, of these small tips can keep you motivated while getting to the bottom of your issues.

You should feel good about yourself inside and out. At this point, you should know your value; no man, woman, or child should be able to tamper with or sway your feelings about yourself.

I wouldn't advise trying to go through this journey alone. Communicate with your family and friends, so they understand the emotional battle ahead. Some days, you'll want to give up, and you'll need a push of encouragement to keep going.

To completely conquer some extreme cases of low self-esteem, a woman may have to completely change her environment. That may consist of getting a new job, moving across town, or even moving out of state in order to completely change your social environment and avoid the clubs you used to go to or the people in your old social circle. Low self-esteem should be taken seriously; just like a person trying to kick a drug addiction, you may have to completely change your normal routine. In some cases, the battle against low self-esteem is one of life or death; extreme measures sometimes have to be taken.

There is nothing worse than being a prisoner in your own body, unable to escape your thoughts. So once you've cleansed yourself from the inside and gotten that much-needed confidence, you need to do everything in your power to keep it that way. People may not like the fact that they can't manipulate you and use you to their advantage. For example, a girl who is shy and timid and who never speaks her mind may lose a lot of friends once she changes for the better. Self-confidence and self-esteem will allow her to begin speaking her mind, as opposed to sitting in silence. No longer afraid to meet new people, she will begin networking and truly start to blossom.

When you've become a new version of yourself, expect a few people to dwindle away from your circle, because they may not like the adopted attitude. Be prepared to embrace change and know that things are changing for the better; let nothing and no one get in the way of gaining your confidence. I will warn you again: There is a thin line, and I do mean *thin* line, between confidence and conceit. Take heed of that and remind yourself to stay humble.

As I was growing up, I never knew how important it was to have peace of mind. However, as you get older, and after all the drama, trials, and tribulations, you'll quickly learn that peace of mind doesn't hold any retail value—it's priceless.

You never know how you may have an impact on someone's life, whether positively or negatively. Do everything in your power to not be the reason a little girl begins to develop low self-esteem. As far back as preschool, I can remember the faces, jokes, and chants I heard when I walked in a room. It took me most of my life to finally conquer my past and shed low self-esteem. We want to prevent the school shootings and the bullying; we want to make it easier for our children today.

I will end this book with a simple rule of thumb: "Do unto others as you would have done unto you." Until next time, ladies—my name is Rena Camille, and this is the end of my journey.

This is your personal journal to help you pinpoint where your self-esteem issues originate from, visually showing you the steps needed to correct those issues. Use this journal to track your progress for the first three months. The first month will be the hardest, requiring lots of changes and adjustments; the second month shouldn't be as strenuous as long as you work on your issues daily and get into a routine; by the third month, you'll be able to see whether you were able to stick to your new routine.

YOUR PERSONAL
JOURNEY

Your Thoughts

_____
_____
_____
_____
_____
_____
_____
_____
_____
_____
_____
_____
_____
_____
_____
_____
_____
_____
_____
_____
_____
_____
_____
_____
_____
_____
_____
_____
_____
_____
_____
_____

Rena Camille

Rena Camille

Draw Your Low Self-Esteem Diagram

List the necessary steps needed to conquer low self-esteem:

-
-
-
-
-
-
-
-
-
-
-
-
-
-
-
-

Month One Progress

Week 1

Rena Camille

Week 2

_____
_____
_____
_____
_____
_____
_____
_____
_____
_____
_____
_____
_____
_____
_____
_____
_____
_____
_____
_____
_____
_____
_____
_____
_____
_____
_____
_____
_____
_____
_____
_____

Rena Camille

Week 3

Rena Camille

Week 4

_____
_____
_____
_____
_____
_____
_____
_____
_____
_____
_____
_____
_____
_____
_____
_____
_____
_____
_____
_____
_____
_____
_____
_____
_____
_____
_____
_____
_____
_____
_____
_____
_____
_____
_____

Rena Camille

Month Two Progress

Week 1

Week 2

_____

Week 3

Rena Camille

Week 4

_____
_____
_____
_____
_____
_____
_____
_____
_____
_____
_____
_____
_____
_____
_____
_____
_____
_____
_____
_____
_____
_____
_____
_____
_____
_____
_____
_____
_____
_____
_____
_____
_____

Month Three Progress

Week 1

Rena Camille

Week 2

_____

_____

_____

_____

_____

_____

_____

_____

_____

_____

_____

_____

_____

_____

_____

_____

_____

_____

_____

_____

_____

_____

_____

_____

_____

_____

_____

_____

_____

_____

_____

_____

_____

_____

_____

Rena Camille

Week 3

Week 4

_____

_____

_____

_____

_____

_____

_____

_____

_____

_____

_____

_____

_____

_____

_____

_____

_____

_____

_____

_____

_____

_____

_____

_____

_____

_____

_____

_____

_____

_____

_____

_____

_____

_____

_____

Rena Camille

_____
_____
_____
_____
_____
_____
_____
_____
_____
_____
_____
_____
_____
_____
_____
_____
_____
_____
_____
_____
_____
_____
_____
_____
_____
_____
_____
_____
_____
_____
_____
_____